Original title:
The Silent Night

Copyright © 2024 Swan Charm
All rights reserved.

Author: Kaido Väinamäe
ISBN HARDBACK: 978-9916-79-342-8
ISBN PAPERBACK: 978-9916-79-343-5
ISBN EBOOK: 978-9916-79-344-2

Echoes of Starlit Peace

In the quiet of the night,
Soft whispers take their flight.
Stars twinkle with gentle grace,
Illuminating this sacred space.

Moonbeams dance on silver lakes,
As the world around us wakes.
Nature holds its breath so still,
Bound by a cosmic thrill.

Every heartbeat feels so clear,
In the vastness, lost our fear.
Echoes of a distant song,
Remind us where we all belong.

Trees sway to the night's soft tune,
Underneath a watchful moon.
Dreams weave through the peaceful air,
Carrying our wishes rare.

In this realm, we find our way,
Underneath the Milky Way.
Hearts united, souls release,
Finding solace, starlit peace.

Stars that Listen

In the quiet of night, they gleam,
Whispers of wishes, a soft, bright beam.
Silent companions, glowing and wise,
Guarding our secrets, under the skies.

Each twinkle a promise, held ever tight,
They guide our hearts, through shadow and light.
Voices are carried on the breath of the air,
In the stillness, they listen, always there.

The Murmurs of Midnight

Midnight unfolds with a soft, cool sigh,
The world is hushed, as stars drift by.
Whispers of shadows dance on the ground,
In this sacred hour, magic is found.

The moon casts her silver, a haunting glow,
Carrying tales from long ago.
In every rustle, in every breeze,
Midnight murmurs, secrets to tease.

Solitude in a Celestial Canvas

Alone with the cosmos, beneath the vast skies,
I find my reflection in the starlit ties.
Each star a brushstroke, a moment to feel,
In the silence of night, the heart learns to heal.

Nebulas swirl with colors so bright,
Painting my dreams in the gentle night light.
In solitude's refuge, I learn to believe,
In the beauty of silence, I learn to perceive.

Dreams Woven in Darkness

In the cloak of the night, dreams softly weave,
Threads of the heart, in shadows perceive.
Tales of tomorrow, in slumber laid bare,
Woven with hope, in the still midnight air.

The fabric of possibility wraps me so tight,
Creating visions that dance in the night.
With every heartbeat, the darkness unfolds,
A tapestry rich with the dreams that it holds.

Reverence of the Night

The stars begin to bloom,
In the velvet skies,
Soft whispers in the gloom,
As the day slowly dies.

Moonlight paints the ground,
Silver beams so pure,
A tranquil, sacred sound,
The heart feels secure.

Creatures hide and play,
In shadows they reside,
Night's gentle ballet,
Where secrets safely hide.

Each breath a soft prayer,
To the darkened skies,
Finding peace somewhere,
As the daylight flies.

Embrace the cool night air,
With dreams that softly spark,
In this world of rare,
We find light in the dark.

A Soft Call from Dusk

The day begins to fade,
Whispers greet the night,
Nature's grand parade,
In softening twilight.

Shadows stretch and yawn,
Colors blend and flow,
A new world is drawn,
Where the gentle dreams grow.

Every star a friend,
Twinkling from afar,
A message they send,
Dusk's sweet, guiding star.

The horizon breathes slow,
With promises untold,
In the afterglow,
The heart feels consoled.

As night takes its throne,
We listen, we trust,
In whispers alone,
The dusk is a must.

Hidden Stories of the Dark

In the shadows where dreams dwell,
Stories wait to unfold,
Silent whispers, a secret spell,
In the dark they're retold.

The moon, a silent guide,
Illuminates the past,
Where forgotten tales abide,
In shadows they are cast.

Time holds its breath tight,
In the depths of the night,
Every flicker of light,
Tells of what feels right.

Paths made of starlit dust,
Lead us to unveil,
The beauty in the trust,
Of stories that prevail.

Within the night's embrace,
Life's mysteries ignite,
In this endless space,
We find our delight.

Beneath the Gaze of Eternity

Stars like diamonds bright,
Gaze upon our plight,
Telling tales of old,
In their shimmering gold.

Beneath the vast expanse,
We ponder and we dream,
Lost in cosmic dance,
Flowing like a stream.

Eternity whispers low,
Secrets held so dear,
In the soft night's glow,
We feel them draw near.

Life, a fleeting spark,
In the grand design,
Yet under the dark,
Our spirits entwine.

With each breath we take,
We touch the divine,
In this quiet wake,
As stars brightly shine.

Beneath the Shimmering Veil of Night

Stars whisper secrets in the dark,
Moonlight dances on the lake's embrace.
Dreams unfold where shadows embark,
Hidden wonders in a silent space.

Winds caress the leaves with grace,
Echoes of starlight fill the air.
Night's embrace, a warm embrace,
Cradles hopes without a care.

A canvas painted with silver hues,
Midnight tales that softly beckon.
In the stillness, the heart renews,
While the world around it lies beckon.

Time melts softly into the deep,
Crickets serenade the gentle breeze.
Within the silence, secrets keep,
And the night whispers with ease.

Beneath the shimmering veil we tread,
Footsteps quiet on the cool grass.
Where the dreams and the starlight spread,
In the dark, we find our path to pass.

Holding the Breath of the Universe

Galaxies swirl in endless flight,
Embers of light stretch far and wide.
In silence, we feel the cosmic bite,
As stars and planets peacefully collide.

Time moves slow, in weightless air,
The quiet hum of creation's song.
Each heartbeat echoes, a vibrant prayer,
In this vast realm where we belong.

Galaxies whisper, stories untold,
Mysteries held in the fabric of night.
We stand in awe, as wonders unfold,
Breathless in the enchanting sight.

Each moment lingers, a fleeting gem,
Holding the breath of the universe tight.
In every heartbeat, whispers of them,
Echo through the canvas of night.

Together we weave a tapestry bright,
In reverence to all that we see.
Holding the breath, dimming the light,
In the stillness, we become free.

The Still Pulse of Midnight

Midnight's pulse, a gentle flow,
In the quiet, a heartbeat near.
Each tick of time begins to slow,
As solace wraps us, crystal clear.

Whispers linger in the cool air,
Stars twinkle in a velvet sea.
In the stillness, we find a prayer,
A moment frozen, wild and free.

Shadows dance on the walls of dreams,
Flickering candles cast soft light.
In the depths, nothing is as it seems,
When wrapped up in the arms of night.

The world outside fades far away,
A cocoon formed by twilight's veil.
In this sanctuary, whispers sway,
As we listen to the nightingale.

In the still pulse, we find our grace,
Holding close to the breath of time.
Midnight's warmth, a soft embrace,
A lullaby, a gentle rhyme.

A Gallery of Dreamscapes Unseen

Canvas wide, with colors bold,
Brushstrokes of wonder paint the sky.
In each corner, stories unfold,
A gallery where dreams can fly.

Whispers of hope, brush against time,
Every hue a fleeting embrace.
In these dreams, we find our rhyme,
In vivid tales, we leave our trace.

Imagined worlds, beyond the reach,
Where fantasies take root and grow.
Through the heart, the soul can teach,
In these spaces, we learn to flow.

Galaxy rivers, with stardust waves,
Serenading the hearts that dare.
In this gallery, spirit braves,
Unseen realms, where we intertwine care.

Dreamscapes beckon, a call to roam,
In this vast expanse, we belong.
Amidst the colors, we find a home,
A dance of creation, a timeless song.

Tranquil Moments Under the Sky

Soft clouds drift in the azure,
Beneath the sun's warm embrace.
Whispers of breeze stir the leaves,
In stillness, time finds its place.

Butterflies dance on bright petals,
Gentle echoes in the air.
Moments linger like sweet honey,
In nature's calm, beyond compare.

Stars peek out as daylight fades,
Moonlight spills on the grassy ground.
Night wraps us in its tender arms,
In silence, solace can be found.

Ripples glide on the peaceful lake,
Reflections of dreams softly gleam.
Hearts unwind in this sanctuary,
Awake inside a lovely dream.

Breath by breath, the world slows down,
Each heartbeat a soothing rhyme.
Under this vast and endless sky,
We bask in the grace of time.

Quietude's Gentle Caress

In the hush of early morning,
Birds sing softly from the trees.
A whisper of the coming day,
Carries with it a gentle breeze.

Misty fog wraps the valley low,
Blanketing all in quiet grace.
The world awakens, slow and sweet,
In this peaceful, sacred space.

Sunlight drips through the branches,
Illuminating paths we tread.
In the warmth of this quiet hour,
Every worry gently shed.

Flowers bloom in silent colors,
Colors radiant under light.
Nature hums a soothing tune,
Inviting us to hold it tight.

Cicadas drone as shadows stretch,
Evening draws near with a sigh.
In tranquility's embrace, we rest,
As the stars begin to spry.

Whispers of a Forgotten Dream

In the stillness of the twilight,
Old memories begin to weave.
Echoes from a time long past,
In the heart, they gently cleave.

Faded dreams like soft shadows,
Drift like smoke through the night air.
Each thought held in a soft embrace,
Creating a sanctuary rare.

Silent laughter, tender moments,
Dance upon the whispering breeze.
Fragments of a life once lived,
Brought back by the swaying trees.

Fleeting glimpses of sweet laughter,
Trail behind like stars at dawn.
In the depths of tranquil silence,
These cherished dreams are never gone.

As the moon bathes the world in silver,
Hope rejuvenates each sigh.
In these whispers of forgotten dreams,
Love endures, it cannot die.

Serene Echoes Beneath the Pines

Beneath tall pines, the shadows play,
Soft whispers dart from tree to tree.
Nature sings a gentle refrain,
In harmony, wild and free.

Dappled sunlight paints the ground,
As soft needles carpet the earth.
Every step brings quiet comfort,
In this place of timeless worth.

Birds flit through branches above,
Echoing laughter through the air.
In the stillness, nature speaks,
Secrets held with tender care.

Lakes shimmer with a gentle luster,
Mirrored skies reflect the peace.
In this haven of solitude,
Worries find a sweet release.

As twilight beckons the day to end,
Stars puncture the vast, inky dome.
Beneath the pines, we find our heart,
In serene echoes, we feel at home.

Nocturnal Reflections in Cool Air

In the dark where shadows play,
Whispers of the night hold sway.
Stars above begin to gleam,
Softly drift on silver stream.

Breezes carry secrets low,
Underneath the moon's soft glow.
Gentle sighs of midnight air,
Nature's voice, a hidden prayer.

Crickets chirp a soothing tune,
Rustling leaves beneath the moon.
Calm descends, the world at rest,
In the stillness, feel the blessed.

Mirrored lakes like glassy eyes,
Reflecting dreams and soft sighs.
Each moment, a treasure rare,
Captured in the cool night air.

Time stands still, a fleeting kiss,
In this night of tranquil bliss.
Let go worries, let them fly,
Underneath the velvet sky.

Whispers in the Moonlight

The moon drapes silver on the ground,
Where quiet secrets softly sound.
Shadows dance with gentle grace,
In this peaceful, hallowed space.

Stars are scattered, bright and clear,
Each a thought we hold so dear.
Breezes hover, brushing skin,
A calming hush where dreams begin.

Night blooms forth, its petals wide,
As echoes of the day subside.
With every sigh, the world unwinds,
In moonlit paths, the heart finds peace.

Crickets sing in rhythmic hum,
Nature's music, sweetly strum.
In this moment, we belong,
Surrounded by the night's soft song.

Whispers float through stillness vast,
Boundless dreams of shadows cast.
In the glow, our spirits soar,
As night reveals what lies in store.

Stillness Beneath the Stars

Barefoot on the cool, soft grass,
Lost in thoughts, where moments pass.
Stars like diamonds twinkle bright,
Guiding dreams through calmest night.

Whispers weave through ancient trees,
Carried softly by the breeze.
A tranquil hush surrounds the air,
Filling hearts with gentle care.

With every breath, a tale unfolds,
In the stillness, life beholds.
Nature's arms, they hold us tight,
Cradled safe in velvet night.

As we gaze at heavens wide,
Hopes and fears so neatly tied.
In the cosmos, we find grace,
Embracing each serene embrace.

Time, a river, flows away,
Underneath the stars we stay.
In this silence, dreams come near,
In the stillness, all is clear.

Echoes of a Quiet Evening

As daylight fades, the silence grows,
In evening's cloak, the stillness flows.
Footsteps soft on winding paths,
Nature's breath, a symphony that lasts.

Colors blend in twilight's hue,
Each moment rich with something new.
In the distance, feelings stir,
Echoes of this world, a gentle blur.

Beneath the sky, so deep and vast,
We find our peace, forgetting fast.
Moments cherished, held so tight,
In the shadows of fading light.

The whispering winds begin to sway,
Carrying worries far away.
Underneath the stars' embrace,
We find solace in this place.

In the quiet, voices meld,
Stories of old, and wishes held.
As night unfolds its tender glow,
We are reminded of love's flow.

Night's Canvas of Peace

Stars twinkle softly in the sky,
Whispers of dreams gently sigh.
Moonlight dances on the trees,
As shadows sway in the cool breeze.

Peace envelops the quiet night,
Crickets sing with pure delight.
The world rests in a warm embrace,
Finding solace in this space.

Ripples kiss the darkened lake,
Time pauses, no heart to break.
In the hush, worries fade away,
Night's canvas beckons to stay.

Softly wrapped in silver light,
Night cradles the stars so bright.
Each moment, a gentle caress,
In silence, we find our rest.

Through the stillness, dreams take flight,
Hopes flicker like candles bright.
Under the vast, starlit dome,
We find peace, we find home.

Enigmatic Silence

In the stillness, secrets weave,
The world whispers, do believe.
Echoes of thoughts, softly tread,
In the silence, stories spread.

A gentle hush blankets the ground,
In this moment, truth is found.
Shadows linger, tales untold,
In the quiet, mysteries unfold.

Beneath the stars, a tranquil vow,
The enigma, sacred now.
Voices unheard, yet felt so near,
In this silence, we draw near.

The rustle of leaves, a fleeting sound,
In the quiet, hearts rebound.
Every glance, a piece of art,
In this silence, we impart.

As night drapes its velvet cloak,
Every breath becomes a stroke.
In this enigmatic bliss,
We find the peace we can't miss.

A Tapestry of Starglow

Woven dreams in the night's embrace,
Stars glimmer in a cosmic space.
Each twinkle tells a tale from old,
In the dark, wonders unfold.

Nebulas swirl in vibrant hues,
Painting skies with celestial blues.
Galaxies spin, an endless flight,
A tapestry of pure delight.

Whispers of starlight guide the way,
In this tapestry, we sway.
Every shine, a spark of hope,
In the vastness, we learn to cope.

Constellations weave our fate,
In this beauty, we meditate.
Through the milky twilight veil,
We ride the stardust, we set sail.

As night unfolds its mystic art,
Starglow dances in the heart.
Together, we bask in the glow,
In this wonder, our spirits grow.

The Stillness Within

In quiet breaths, the world dissolves,
In gentle peace, our hearts evolve.
The chaos fades, a whisper free,
In the stillness, we find 'me'.

Moments pause, like soft-spun silk,
Every heartbeat, a glass of milk.
The mind quiets, thoughts drift away,
In the stillness, we hear the play.

Waves of calm lap at the shore,
In this still peace, we lose the roar.
Nature sings a lullaby sweet,
Here, the spirit feels complete.

Every sigh, a breath of grace,
In the stillness, we embrace.
A sanctuary built within,
Where the journey can begin.

Through the shadows, light will break,
In this stillness, we awake.
Finding depth, the truth we cling,
In the quiet, our souls will sing.

Night's Sacred Refuge

In shadows deep, the stillness reigns,
Under the stars, where silence gains.
Whispers of dreams weave through the air,
A gentle embrace, a secret prayer.

Moonlight dances on tranquil lakes,
Painting the world as daylight breaks.
Crickets sing sweet lullabies,
While time fades softly under night skies.

Cool breezes carry a calming sigh,
As the weary wanderers pass by.
In the cocoon of night, we find
A solace, tender, peace entwined.

Each moment lingers, a fleeting spark,
In this sacred refuge, free from the dark.
Hearts merge with the calm, a soothing balm,
Finding our way in this perfect calm.

Awash in the glow of the silver light,
We breathe in the magic, embrace the night.
With every heartbeat, the world feels right,
In Night's Sacred Refuge, pure delight.

Serenity Wrapped in Night

Stars twinkle softly, a gentle glance,
In the quiet, we find our chance.
Wrapped in the fabric of velvet skies,
Serenity blooms as the day dies.

Whispers of nature in harmony flow,
As the moon casts shadows, a soft glow.
Crickets serenade the world asleep,
In the stillness, our secrets we keep.

The world in repose, a canvas clear,
With every heartbeat, our dreams draw near.
In this tranquil hour, we let go,
Finding our peace in the soft night's show.

Breath by breath, we trace the night,
In every pause, we find the light.
Serenity wrapped in night's embrace,
A gentle reminder of our place.

As shadows dance in the silver hue,
The heart opens wide to the view.
Finding solace, we feel reborn,
In Serenity Wrapped, our spirits adorn.

Echoes of Tranquility

In the night, echoes softly blend,
Carrying whispers that never end.
A tranquil breath, the world at standstill,
Lost in the magic that night fulfills.

Moonbeams shimmer, dancing on trees,
Caressing the leaves with the sweetest tease.
Each rustling sound, a story unfolds,
In echoes of tranquility, peace it holds.

Stars weave patterns, a tapestry bright,
Guiding the dreamers through the night.
In the silence, we hear the call,
Of ancient murmurs, a wisdom for all.

Wrapped in the arms of the cool night air,
Every worry fades without a care.
With each heartbeat, a rhythm we keep,
In echoes of solace, softly we sleep.

The world outside slips far away,
In tranquility's arms, we wish to stay.
Let the night cradle our weary souls,
In the embrace of silence, we are whole.

Beneath the Veil of Twilight

Beneath the veil, the twilight glows,
A hush settles in, as daylight slows.
Colors fade softly in the evening light,
Welcoming dreams that take their flight.

Crimson and gold, the sky's attire,
Kindling the heart's long-lost desire.
With every star that begins to gleam,
We gather our wishes, we whisper a dream.

The horizon blurs in a dreamy haze,
As shadows cradle the end of days.
In this gentle pause, our spirits rise,
Beneath the veil, we claim the skies.

Cool breezes brush past like soft caress,
In twilight's embrace, we find our rest.
Whispers of night call us to explore,
The magic that lies behind every door.

With every breath, we feel the change,
A promise of peace, a gentle exchange.
In twilight's charm, we softly entwine,
Beneath the veil, forever divine.

Nocturnal Reveries

In shadows deep, the silence breathes,
A world unfolds beneath the leaves.
Stars whisper tales of distant lands,
As moonlight spills through gentle hands.

Dreams take flight on velvet wings,
In night's embrace, the heartstrings sing.
Every glimpse of starlit skies,
Holds secrets known to wandering eyes.

Softly flows the river's song,
Where whispers of the night belong.
Beneath the veil of velvet dark,
The soul ignites with every spark.

Time dissolves in this twilight space,
As shadows dance with haunting grace.
In quiet realms, we lose our way,
And find ourselves in shades of gray.

Oh, cherish these nocturnal hours,
Where dreams awaken hidden powers.
In every sigh, a secret hides,
Within the night, the magic bides.

Secrets in the Twilight Glow

The evening sighs, a soft embrace,
As twilight paints the sky with grace.
Whispers linger on the breeze,
Secrets dwelling among the trees.

Glimmers sparkle, soft and shy,
As fireflies dance, they light the sky.
Each moment wrapped in hushed delight,
Beneath the stars, the world feels right.

Such dreams awaken in this hour,
In shadows cast by twilight's power.
Each heartbeat finds its rhythm slow,
In the magic of the twilight glow.

Gentle echoes call our name,
In the night, we play a game.
With whispered secrets, soft and low,
We dive into this twilight glow.

Together, lost in night's embrace,
We follow paths that time won't trace.
In every breath, a love will grow,
Amid the secrets of twilight's flow.

Velvet Whispers of Night

In velvet whispers, night unfolds,
With tales of dreams and secrets told.
A gentle hush blankets the land,
As starlit fingers brush the sand.

Every shadow holds a sigh,
Cradled softly by the sky.
In the darkness, magic hums,
While distant, heartfelt music strums.

The moonlight bathes the world in grace,
A tender touch, a warm embrace.
Silent moments spin and twirl,
As dreams emerge and softly swirl.

Velvet skies invite us near,
To whisper secrets we hold dear.
In every glimmer, stars ignite,
The wonder of the velvet night.

So let us linger, hand in hand,
And breathe the dreams that night has planned.
In whispered tones, our hearts delight,
In the soft velvet of the night.

A Journey through Hushed Dreams

In slumber's arms, we gently glide,
Through whispered paths where secrets hide.
A journey waits beyond our sight,
In the silence of velvet night.

Stars beckon softly, dreams take flight,
Guided by the moon so bright.
Each breath a step, each thought a seam,
We weave the fabric of our dream.

In quiet corners, shadows play,
Where night unfolds in shades of gray.
With every heartbeat, time stands still,
As night awakens dreams to fill.

Through meadows lush and starlit seas,
Among the sighs of rustling trees.
We wander on this gentle stream,
Embracing all the hush of dreams.

So come and dance in twilight's glow,
Where every whisper starts to flow.
In the embrace of night's soft hands,
We find our peace in dreamland's sands.

Echoes of the Night's Cool Embrace

Whispers linger in the dark,
Stars alight, a cosmic spark.
Moonlight dances on the stream,
Holding tight each fleeting dream.

Shadows stretch and softly sigh,
Crickets sing, the night slips by.
Branches sway in gentle tune,
Beneath the watchful, silver moon.

In the stillness, secrets hide,
Time unwinds, a fleeting ride.
Breath of night, cool and deep,
Cradling thoughts like dreams in sleep.

Echoes of a long-lost song,
Carried gently, where they belong.
In the night's embrace, we find,
Comfort wrapped in shadows blind.

Serenity, a quiet grace,
In the folds of night's own face.
Echoes weave through every sound,
In that peace, our hearts are bound.

A Subtle Brush with Infinity

Glimmers dance in endless space,
Time and light begin their chase.
Moments glimpse what lies beyond,
Whispers of the unseen bond.

As we wander through the haze,
Every heartbeat, a fleeting phase.
Stars align in perfect rhyme,
Echoing the pulse of time.

A breath held tight in quiet awe,
Unraveled truths we gently draw.
Each connection, a fragile thread,
Binding dreams of what's unsaid.

The night unveils its subtle art,
Painting shadows on the heart.
With each stroke, we realize,
Infinity's a sweet disguise.

Moments shimmer, soft and rare,
Prompting us to stop and stare.
In the vastness, we find our place,
A brush with time's eternal grace.

When Time Takes a Breather

In a world of racing feet,
Moments pause, a heartbeat sweet.
Sunsets linger, colors blend,
Time leans back, a gentle friend.

Silent whispers fill the air,
Thoughts emerge anew, laid bare.
Days drift softly, shadows sway,
In the stillness, dreams can play.

Clocks relent, they slow their toll,
As we search to feel more whole.
Nature holds its breath in tune,
Time exhaled beneath the moon.

Sweet nostalgia, soft and bright,
Wraps around us like the night.
In these moments, peace we find,
When time stops, we unwind.

Colors bloom in gentle grace,
Echoes linger, time and space.
When we pause, embrace the now,
Time takes breath, we take a bow.

Paths Embroidered with Shadows

Winding trails beneath the trees,
Whispers carried by the breeze.
Footsteps trace a secret beat,
Paths embroidered, bittersweet.

Sunlight filters through the leaves,
In the shade, a heart believes.
Every shadow tells a tale,
Of wanderers who set their sail.

In the quiet, stories bloom,
Echoing the stillness' loom.
Beneath the weight of whispered dreams,
Life unfolds in tangled seams.

Each step taken, echoes past,
Roots entwined, our fates are cast.
Carving journeys through the night,
Every path, a dance of light.

With every turn, we face the dark,
Finding courage, leaving mark.
Paths embroidered with love's glow,
In the shadows, we all grow.

Stars are Secrets Untold

In the velvet sky they gleam,
Whispers of dreams and old tales.
Each spark a wish, it would seem,
Carrying hope as night pales.

Hidden truths they softly show,
In silence, their stories flow.
Light years apart, yet so near,
In the stillness, their songs we hear.

A tapestry of lights above,
Stitching the night with sweet love.
Silent compadres in the dark,
Guiding the heart, igniting a spark.

As we gaze with wonder and awe,
Revealing beauty in every flaw.
Stars are secrets the night has told,
Whispering stories of brave and bold.

So we linger and watch them play,
Following dreams that drift away.
In the cosmos, where wishes reside,
Stars become hopes that never hide.

Hushed Reveries of Winter

Snowflakes dance on whispering winds,
Blanketing earth in quiet grace.
Each flake tells where journey begins,
In the stillness, time leaves no trace.

Frosted branches, a shimmering sight,
Imbued with secrets of the night.
Every shadow cast so deep,
Inviting dreams, inviting sleep.

A soft glow of the moonlight's glow,
Kissing the world with a tender touch.
Lost in thoughts, where memories flow,
Winter's embrace, so soft and much.

Silent woods in slumber profound,
Echo the silence, a sacred sound.
Nature whispers, calm and discreet,
Drawing us close to winter's heartbeat.

In this season, we find our peace,
Moments linger, and worries cease.
Wrapped in the hush of the cold air,
We find solace beyond compare.

Calmness Wrapped in Frost

In the quiet morn, the world sighs,
Veils of frost upon the ground.
A gentle hush as daylight tries,
To wrap us in beauty profound.

Breath of winter, crisp and clear,
Painting landscapes with its wand.
Each glimmering crystal, like a tear,
Mends the heart, as we respond.

Whispers of nature greet the dawn,
As trees wear coats of brilliant white.
In this stillness, our fears are gone,
In the calm, our spirits take flight.

Footsteps crunch on frozen trails,
Echoing softly in the air.
Every breath abounds and sails,
In embrace of winter's fair.

Calmness rests in this frosted space,
Nature's lullaby, a serenade.
In such moments, we find our place,
Wrapped in warmth that won't soon fade.

Night's Gentle Breath

The night descends with a soft sigh,
Wrapping the world in starlit grace.
A tender hush under the sky,
Embracing dreams that softly trace.

Shadows pool in corners deep,
While the moon lets its silver stream.
The world around begins to sleep,
Caught in the fabric of a dream.

Crickets sing their lullaby,
Notes carried on the evening air.
Gentle winds whisper and sigh,
Telling secrets, a love affair.

Every twinkle, a soft caress,
Embracing hearts with silent charms.
In the stillness, we find our rest,
Held in night's loving arms.

As shadows play and moments blend,
Softly folding into the night.
In this tranquil space, we mend,
With night's gentle breath, taking flight.

Luminous Whispers in the Black

In shadows deep, where silence stays,
A flicker glows, the night obeys.
Whispers dance on velvet air,
Their light a balm, a gentle prayer.

Stars twinkle in the vast unknown,
A tapestry of dreams well sewn.
Each shimmer a secret softly shared,
In the heart of darkness, hope is bared.

Moonlight spills on pathways bright,
Guiding souls through the still of night.
A symphony of slow and soft,
In quietude, the spirit's loft.

Eclipsed wishes find their way,
Amidst the night, they long to stay.
With every breath, the world feels wide,
In luminous whispers, dreams abide.

So take my hand, in shadows deep,
Where secrets sigh and silence weeps.
Together we'll chase the fleeting light,
In luminous whispers, hearts ignite.

Serenity Found in Hushed Spaces

In corners soft, where whispers dwell,
A peaceful quiet, a gentle spell.
The world outside begins to fade,
In the hush, sweet calm is laid.

Stillness wraps the weary mind,
In these moments, solace kind.
A sigh escapes the troubled heart,
In hushed spaces, fears depart.

Every breath, a tender pause,
Embraced by night, our silent laws.
Nature's lullaby begins to play,
Cradled in dreams, we drift away.

Soft light falls on sleeping trees,
Swaying gently in the breeze.
The world does turn, yet we find peace,
In whispered breaths, our cares release.

Time stands still, in realms unseen,
A gentle gaze where hearts convene.
In hushed spaces, love will grow,
Serenity found, our spirits flow.

Somnolent Melodies of the Night

In the stillness, a lullaby plays,
Night's soft tunes weave through the grays.
Gentle echoes of dreams take flight,
Somnolent melodies guide the night.

Whispers float on moonlit streams,
Carrying the hopes of quiet dreams.
With every note, the shadows sigh,
As stars serenade the velvet sky.

A tranquil hum, the world asleep,
In this slumber, secrets keep.
The crickets sing their twilight song,
In their chorus, we all belong.

In the hush, our worries fade,
The soothing tune of twilight's shade.
Wrapped in warmth, the night unfolds,
Somnolent stories quietly told.

Hear the symphony of dreams arise,
Underneath the sprawling skies.
A dance of shadows, gently bright,
In somnolent melodies, love takes flight.

A Dreamer's Wanderlust in Darkness

In the quiet void of endless night,
A dreamer wanders, seeking light.
Through galaxies where wishes twirl,
A pulse of hope begins to swirl.

With each heartbeat, the stars align,
Drawing paths through space and time.
The darkness holds a thousand doors,
A dreamer's heart forever soars.

Adventurous visions beckon near,
In shadows deep, there's naught to fear.
A tapestry of night unfolds,
In whispered tales, the cosmos holds.

With every step, the journey grows,
Across the realms where stardust flows.
In dreaming dreams, the spirit learns,
A wanderer's heart forever yearns.

And as the moonlit paths are traced,
In darkened skies, we find our place.
Unraveled in the deep abyss,
A dreamer's wanderlust, pure bliss.

Dreams Wrapped in Midnight's Veil

In shadows deep, where whispers lie,
The stars ignite the velvet sky.
Each dream a spark, a fleeting flight,
Wrapped in the cloak of soothing night.

Gentle breezes weave through trees,
Carrying tales on midnight's breeze.
With every sigh, a wish takes form,
In this stillness, hearts stay warm.

Moonlit paths invite us near,
To dance with thoughts that disappear.
In the silence, secrets blend,
Where every night, new dreams ascend.

The world slows down, a tender spell,
In the deep dark, where echoes dwell.
Here time suspends its endless chase,
And we embrace this sacred space.

As dawn whispers, dreams take flight,
But for now, we hold the night.
In midnight's veil, we find our peace,
With every moment, sweet release.

The Calm Before the Dawn's Arrival

A hush descends, the world holds breath,
In twilight's arms, we gather depth.
The stars align, a gentle glow,
As night prepares to end its show.

Whispers float on the cooling air,
Time stands still, a moment rare.
The universe takes a breath anew,
In colors soft, both bright and blue.

Shadows creep as thoughts align,
In this stillness, dreams entwine.
The moon bids farewell to the night,
Preparing for the sun's first light.

Horizon blushes, mixing hues,
A canvas fresh, with vibrant views.
The calm before the heat of day,
A fleeting pause before the sway.

In silence lingers sweet refrain,
Remnants of night like softest rain.
As we await the day's embrace,
We find our strength, our hidden grace.

Hushed Lullabies of the Cosmos

In the cradle of stars, soft songs play,
Lullabies wrap us, night turns to day.
Galaxies twirl in a dreamy spin,
Holding our hopes, a warm embrace within.

With every twinkle, a tale unfolds,
Of ancient whispers and secrets old.
The cosmos hums with a gentle tune,
Guiding our hearts by the light of the moon.

Nebulas blush with a painter's brush,
In the quiet of night, we feel the hush.
Each note a wish floated on high,
A serenade sung by the endless sky.

The echoes of space embrace our souls,
As starlit dreams become our goals.
In silent harmony, we drift and sway,
To the lullabies that the night will play.

As dawn approaches, these songs won't fade,
For in our hearts, their magic's made.
A melody etched in the fabric of time,
In hushed whispers, life's rhythm and rhyme.

Night's Soft Sugarcoat

The night descends like a gentle sigh,
Wrapped in the sweetness of a starry sky.
Every corner glimmers, a hidden treat,
In twilight's embrace, the world feels complete.

Soft shadows dance on the pavement cool,
As moonbeams shimmer, a silvery pool.
Each streetlamp flickers, a guiding flame,
In this quiet hour, the world feels tame.

Whispers of dreams float on the breeze,
Carried away through the swaying trees.
In the hush, every moment swells,
As night casts its spell, where magic dwells.

With every heartbeat, sweetness flows,
In the silent night, our spirit glows.
Wrapped in a blanket of starry delight,
We savor the treasures that come with the night.

As dawn approaches, this sweetness remains,
A sugarcoat of dreams and soft refrains.
In the heart of night, we'll always reside,
Finding comfort and joy in the evening tide.

A Symphony of Sighs

In shadows deep, where echoes play,
Soft whispers gather at the end of day.
Each breath a note, a gentle song,
A symphony of sighs that lingers long.

The stars above blink in agree,
Their light a hush, so tenderly.
With every twinkle, stories weave,
Of hopes and dreams that never leave.

Moonlit paths adorned in grace,
Guide weary hearts to a tranquil space.
In the night, a melody flows,
As nature's breath sings soft and low.

Hands reach out in the quiet night,
Finding solace in shared light.
Together we dance to the softest tune,
Under the gaze of the watchful moon.

As dawn draws near, the sighs retreat,
Yet in their wake, our hearts still beat.
For in this night, we found our way,
A symphony of sighs that will not fade away.

Whispered Dreams in the Dark

In the quiet corners where shadows dwell,
Whispered dreams weave a secret spell.
With every flicker, a hope ignites,
In the tapestry of endless nights.

Stars above, like tales untold,
Glimmer softly, bright yet cold.
They listen close to wishes spun,
In the fabric of dusk, where journeys run.

Beneath the veil of the silent sky,
Hearts take flight as the moments fly.
Echoes of laughter, sweet and clear,
In whispered dreams, we hold them dear.

Through the haze of sleep, we wander free,
Exploring realms of possibility.
Each heartbeat syncs to a timeless flow,
In the dark, our spirits glow.

As night gives way to morning light,
The dreams dissolve, yet take their flight.
In whispered thoughts, they find their place,
Illuminating our waking grace.

The Heartbeat of Quietude

In stillness deep, a heartbeat grows,
Whispers of peace where the soft wind blows.
Calm waters reflect the gentle sigh,
As nature's pulse echoes, low and high.

Leaves dance lightly on the morning breeze,
With every flutter, the spirit frees.
A moment cherished, a breath held tight,
In the heartbeat of quietude, pure delight.

Mountains stand as guardians of time,
Holding secrets in their silent rhyme.
Each dawn unveils a world new-born,
In tranquil spaces, no need to mourn.

Time slows down as the shadows blend,
Creating softness, around each bend.
In the still air, we hear the call,
Of the heartbeat of quietude, holding us all.

As dusk descends, the colors fade,
Yet the heart remains, unafraid.
For in each moment, we truly find,
The pulse of life, both gentle and kind.

Lullabies of the Evening

In the hush of twilight, a song begins,
Lullabies wrapped in the evening's spin.
Softly they echo through the air,
Bringing comfort and gentle care.

The world slows down, the day takes flight,
As stars awake in the velvet night.
Their glow sings sweetly, a soothing balm,
Caressing the heart with a touch of calm.

Breezes whisper through the trees,
Carrying tales on the sighing leaves.
In every rustle, a gentle tone,
Lullabies of the evening, whispering home.

Moonlight dances on the sleeping ground,
Painting dreams with a silver sound.
Every heartbeat finds its place,
In lullabies of love and grace.

As night embraces the weary day,
In dreams we wander, lose the way.
Yet in these songs, we find our rest,
In the lullabies, our souls are blessed.

The Stillness Between Heartbeats

In the hush where silence lingers,
Time drifts softly, a feathered sigh.
Moments pause on fragile fingers,
While echoes of whispers gently fly.

Life's rhythm plays a muted song,
Tension woven into each breath.
Between the heartbeats, I belong,
Where shadows dance with fleeting depth.

Oh, the space where dreams reside,
Holding secrets not yet told.
In stillness, all the worlds collide,
As warmth embraces the evening cold.

Ghostly murmurs fill the air,
Painting visions of what may be.
In the stillness, a subtle flare,
Igniting hope, serene and free.

In the quiet, find your way,
To the pulse that draws you near.
In heartbeats lost, we softly sway,
Life unfurling, crystal clear.

Celestial Serenade of the Unseen

Underneath a velvet sky,
Stars weave tales in whispered light.
Each twinkle, a heartfelt sigh,
A serenade that begins at night.

Galaxies spin, a cosmic dance,
In silence, they twirl and glide.
In this moment, I take a chance,
To lose myself in the vast cosmic tide.

Constellations map a hidden grace,
Stories shared in radiant hues.
Every flicker, a warm embrace,
Guiding the souls that seek the muse.

The moonbeams kiss the sleeping earth,
Cradling dreams with their gentle glow.
In this night, we find our worth,
Under the spell of the starlit show.

Harmony hums, celestial and grand,
Resonating in the depths of the heart.
In this music, I understand,
We are woven into the cosmic art.

Embracing the Night's Gentle Touch

As twilight falls, a whispering breeze,
Cocooning the day in gentle shrouds.
The night arrives with tender ease,
Embracing the world without crowds.

Moonlit trails that softly glow,
Draw us into their tranquil fold.
Each step echoes, pacing slow,
As stories unravel, quietly told.

Stars sprinkle secrets in the dark,
Illuminating paths unseen.
Every spark ignites a new spark,
Creating visions of what might have been.

Wrapped in shadows, I find my peace,
The world outside drifts far away.
In the stillness, worries cease,
And dreams unravel in soft array.

A lullaby of crickets sings,
To cradle souls in night's embrace.
In this moment, the spirit springs,
Finding sanctuary in tranquil space.

Silent Starlight on Slumbering Streets

Beneath the cloak of a starry night,
Streets whisper tales of bygone hours.
Silent echoes, soft and bright,
As moonlight bathes the slumbering flowers.

Each shadow stretches, yawning wide,
Dreams meander through corners small.
In this quiet, there's nowhere to hide,
Where time dances, and wishes call.

The hum of night wraps around me tight,
Holding secrets, both old and new.
In the stillness, there shines a light,
A beacon that speaks to hearts so true.

Stars align in the open sky,
Glistening jewels on a canvas vast.
In their gaze, I can't deny,
A connection to the shadows cast.

Through the silence, a promise forms,
That beauty lies in every scene.
In slumbering streets, beneath the storms,
We find solace in the unseen.

Whispers of the Moonlit Hour

In the hush of night, soft voices sigh,
Beneath the silver glow, shadows lie.
Winds carry tales, ancient and true,
Painting the dark with a mystical hue.

Stars blink slowly, in waltz with the breeze,
As time stands still, our spirits tease.
Dreams take flight on wings of delight,
Cradled gently by the moon's soft light.

Each fluttering heart, a whisper's plea,
In the silence, we find serenity.
Stories unfold, under night's embrace,
In the tender shadows, we find our place.

Echoes of laughter, the night air holds,
Woven in memories, in whispers untold.
With every moment, we dance through the night,
Underneath the watchful, celestial light.

Beneath the moon's gaze, we breathe in peace,
Finding our solace, as moments cease.
Together we linger, in harmony's flow,
In the whispers of night, our spirits grow.

Shimmering Stillness Beneath the Stars

In the still of night, the world holds its breath,
Wrapped in silence, as shadows bequeath.
Stars flicker like jewels, scattered afar,
Lighting our dreams, like a guiding star.

Whispers of echoes drift soft through the trees,
Carried by breezes that sing with such ease.
Each shimmer above, a story unfolds,
In the vastness of space, our hearts break the mold.

Moonlit reflections dance on the lake,
Mirroring secrets, as stillness awakes.
We pause for a moment, lost in the night,
Finding our truth in the softest of light.

Dreamers in shadows, with hopes that ignite,
In shimmering stillness, we chase the twilight.
Each heartbeat a rhythm, beneath starry skies,
In unspoken wonders, our spirits will rise.

As night drapes the earth, we rest and renew,
Bound by the magic, in the night's gentle hue.
Together in silence, our hearts open wide,
In shimmering stillness, forever we bide.

Tranquil Embrace of Shadowed Skies

Under the cloak of the shadowed skies,
Quiet embraces where the soft silence lies.
Moonbeams whisper, serenading the night,
Wrapping the world in a blanket of light.

Gentle are moments, as time drifts so slow,
In tranquil reflections, our spirits will flow.
Stars above witness our tales yet to weave,
In the embrace of night, we tenderly believe.

Breath in the stillness, let worries dissolve,
In the soft shadows, our hearts will evolve.
Crickets are singing, a nocturnal tune,
Swirling around us, under the moon.

With each twinkling light, dreams unfurl wide,
In the tranquil embrace, our fears we abide.
A dance with the night, where the heart learns to soar,
In the shadowed skies, we awaken once more.

Together in silence, we roam infinite lands,
Painting our futures with delicate hands.
In the quiet of night, the world feels so right,
In tranquil embrace, we cherish the light.

Echoes of Serenity in Darkness

In the depth of night, shadows softly call,
Echoes of peace, in the silence, we fall.
Stars weave their magic, in radiant threads,
Guiding our dreams, where the heart gently treads.

Each heartbeat a whisper, in the grand cosmic dance,
Wrapped in serenity, we embrace the chance.
Moonlight's caress on forgotten trails,
In the fabric of night, our spirit prevails.

As darkness unfolds, our worries take flight,
Carried away to the depths of the night.
In the stillness, we linger, creating our space,
In echoes of serenity, our souls find grace.

The world fades away, beneath the vast sky,
In the hush of the night, we learn how to fly.
Stars blink in harmony, a celestial choir,
Lighting our paths with an endless fire.

With every small sigh, we deepen our trust,
In darkness, we gather, our dreams turn to dust.
In echoes of silence, we unravel the night,
Embracing the shadows, we find our true light.

Whispers of Wistfulness

In a garden of dreams, softly we sigh,
Petals drift gently, under twilight's eye.
Faint echoes linger, of laughter once shared,
Memories whisper, in the cool evening air.

Stars twinkle lightly, as shadows draw near,
Wistful reflections, cradle all we hold dear.
Underneath the moon, we find solace anew,
The heart speaks in silence, in a language so true.

Moments like petals, fall softly away,
We gather the warmth, as night blankets day.
In the hush of the eve, our spirits take flight,
Whispers of wistfulness, dance in the night.

Each glance is a story, each sigh, a sweet song,
Time slips like water, where does it belong?
Beneath this starlit sky, we sigh and we dream,
In the garden of thoughts, we flow like a stream.

The dawn will awaken but let us not haste,
For the waves of our hearts, cannot be replaced.
In dreams we will wander, our spirits entwined,
Whispers of wistfulness, by love we're defined.

Illuminated by Stardust

Glistening night skies, a canvas so grand,
Flecks of bright stardust, sprinkle the land.
Each twinkle a wish, whispered soft in the air,
Illuminated bliss, a celestial affair.

Wandering souls beneath, the cosmic glow,
Drawn to the magic, where dreams freely flow.
In the hush of the night, secrets take flight,
Illuminated by stardust, hearts burn bright.

Galaxies twirling, in timeless embrace,
We trace silver lines, through the vastness of space.
Comets in motion, a dance with the moon,
Illuminated by stardust, we sway to its tune.

Whispers of the cosmos, wrapped in the light,
Holding our hopes, through the deep velvet night.
Each star a reminder, we're never alone,
Illuminated paths, lead us back home.

Awake in the magic, our spirits ascend,
Bound by the stardust, love knows no end.
In the shimmer of night, we'll always find trust,
For we are the dreamers, illuminated by stardust.

Shadows of Forgotten Echoes

In the corners of time, where silence does creep,
Shadows of echoes, find voices to keep.
Memories tangled, in webs of the past,
Fleeting moments, too precious to last.

Forgotten whispers, linger in the gloom,
Shadows drawing near, a soft, dark perfume.
In the stillness of night, the heart learns to weep,
For shadows of echoes, together we'll seep.

Each step we've taken, a footfall of grace,
Carving our stories, time cannot erase.
In the twilight, reflections quietly stir,
Shadows of forgotten echoes, memories blur.

Faint laughter dances, through corridors of dreams,
The glow of the past, in soft golden beams.
With each passing whisper, we find and we lose,
Shadows of echoes, our hearts choose to cruise.

As night drifts away, and dawn breaks the spell,
Echoes fade gently, like the toll of a bell.
Yet in every shadow, a moment stays bright,
Shadows of forgotten echoes, linger in light.

Night's Timeless Poise

Under the blanket of the deep velvet night,
Stars hum a lullaby, soft and polite.
Whispers of twilight play sweet on the breeze,
As moonlight dances through the trembling trees.

Gentle are the minutes, like dreams in a sigh,
Bathed in the stillness, where shadows can fly.
Each heartbeat a promise, in the hush of the dark,
Night's timeless poise, leaves a gentle mark.

Reflections of wisdom, in the depths of the sky,
Moonbeams like kisses, from the heavens up high.
In every soft corner, where silence will linger,
Night holds its magic, wrapped tight in its finger.

Stars flicker softly, as worlds intertwine,
A tapestry woven, where dreams intertwine.
In the heart of the night, we float like a dream,
Night's timeless poise, a celestial seam.

As dawn gently beckons, we whisper goodbye,
But night's gentle poise, will never truly die.
In shadows and echoes, it lives on and on,
A dance of existence, from dusk until dawn.

A Canvas of Calm Amidst the Darkness

In the hush where shadows creep,
Stars awaken, secrets keep.
Whispers dance on moonlit streams,
Painting peace in silver beams.

Gentle winds caress the trees,
Rustling leaves, a symphony.
Night unfolds in soft embrace,
A tranquil heart, a sacred space.

Dreams take flight on velvet skies,
Hope ignites as night complies.
With each breath, a world reborn,
New hues rise with every dawn.

Glistening light on dewy grass,
Time flows gently, moments pass.
A canvas vast, serene and bright,
Amidst the calm, we find our light.

Murmurs of the Cosmic Embrace

Galaxies twirl in silent flight,
Twinkling whispers, pure delight.
Nebulae bloom in colors bold,
Stories of the stars foretold.

Echoes of time drift through the void,
Cosmic rhythms, beauty enjoyed.
Each heartbeat syncs with the vast unknown,
In the cosmos, we are not alone.

Celestial winds blow soft and clear,
Guiding dreams, erasing fear.
Beneath the skies, we yearn to roam,
In stardust trails, we find our home.

With every glance, the heavens sigh,
Veils of mystery, deep and high.
Murmurs of love in the endless night,
Embrace the cosmos, feel its light.

Cradled in the Arms of the Night

Softly nestled in twilight's glow,
Dreams whisper where the shadows flow.
Moonbeams cradle our gentle sighs,
In the night, our spirit flies.

Starlit paths weave stories bold,
Comfort found in tales retold.
Nature's hymn plays sweet and low,
Guiding hearts where moonbeams go.

Wrapped in warmth, the world slows down,
Dew-kissed grass, a velvet crown.
Each heartbeat syncs with night's embrace,
Cradled close in starlit space.

The night unveils its secret charms,
With every breath, we find our calm.
In the dark, there's peace to find,
Cradled gently, heart aligned.

Enigmas of the Dusk

As daylight wanes, the colors blend,
Mysteries rise, beginnings end.
Whispers linger in the fading light,
An enigma brews, soft and bright.

Shadows stretch with playful grace,
Dancing dreams, a sacred space.
Nightbird calls, the secret tune,
Underneath the harvest moon.

Twilight's brush paints skies of gold,
Stories woven, secrets told.
Each star a note in the cosmic song,
Belonging where we all are strong.

In dusk's embrace, we find our way,
Glimmers of hope at the end of day.
Enigmas of life, so sweet and true,
In the dusky hues, I find you.

Moonlit Solitude

In the stillness of night, I gaze,
The silver moon casts soothing rays.
Whispers of the wind softly sigh,
As stars twinkle in the quiet sky.

Shadows dance beneath the trees,
Carried softly on the breeze.
Alone but not lonely, I find peace,
In nature's embrace, my worries cease.

Reflections on the water's face,
Invite my mind to a sacred space.
The world fades as dreams take flight,
In the heart of this tranquil night.

Each star a story yet untold,
Secrets of the universe unfold.
Under this dome, I close my eyes,
Embracing the magic of moonlit skies.

Time stands still, moments extend,
In solitude, I find a friend.
The night whispers ancient lore,
Promising there's always more.

A Blanketed World at Dusk

As daylight fades, the colors blend,
A canvas where twilight starts to mend.
Golden hues give way to gray,
As shadows stretch and softly play.

Blankets of mist begin to rise,
Covering earth with soft, tender sighs.
The sun dips low, its warmth withdraws,
While silence wraps the world in claws.

Fleeting moments, the day retreats,
Nature sighs as darkness greets.
Stars shyly peek from their hidden places,
Glimmers of light in shadowed spaces.

A stillness settles over the land,
Every creature hushed, taking a stand.
The night wraps tight, a comforting hand,
In this tranquil, serene, and sacred strand.

While dusk embraces the fading sun,
A silent promise, the day is done.
Tomorrow brings a brand new start,
But for now, I savor dusk's sweet heart.

Velvet Skies of Reflection

Beneath the stretch of velvet night,
I pause to ponder, lost in light.
As galaxies spin in silent dance,
Each star invites a thoughtful glance.

Clouds drift slowly on the breeze,
Whispers of dreams bring me to ease.
In the expanse, my thoughts take flight,
Eclipsing worries, releasing fright.

Time suspends, moments expand,
The universe cradles my outstretched hand.
In reflection, I discover grace,
Embraced by the starlit space.

Each twinkle a mirror, a chance to see,
The depths of my soul, wild and free.
Lost in wonder, beneath the glow,
The velvet sky teaches me to grow.

In quiet reverie, I seek and find,
Connection to all that's intertwined.
The night reveals what daylight hides,
In velvet skies, my spirit glides.

Twilight's Tender Touch

Mellow hues of pink and gold,
In twilight's light, stories are told.
The horizon dips, a warm embrace,
As day slips quietly into space.

Soft whispers float on evening air,
Nature sings without a care.
The world, aglow with gentle grace,
Welcomes shadows, creating a space.

Each moment a brushstroke divine,
Crafted by a hand so fine.
In twilight's glow, hearts intertwine,
As silence blankets, warm and benign.

Stars awaken, shyly they gleam,
Reflections of hopes, a tranquil dream.
In this hour, magic is spun,
As twilight dances with the sun.

The embrace of dusk, soft and sweet,
Whispers of solace, a heartbeat.
In twilight's touch, I find my way,
Guided gently into the fray.

A Canvas of Nightfall

The sky drapes blue with fading light,
Stars emerge, twinkling bright.
Whispers of dusk serenade the air,
Night's gentle brush strokes everywhere.

Silhouettes dance in tranquil hush,
Moonrise brings a silvery blush.
Shadows stretch and entwine,
In the embrace of twilight's design.

Nature holds its breath so still,
As dreams emerge, hearts begin to thrill.
A tapestry woven with every sigh,
Under the vast and watchful sky.

With every glimmer, secrets unfold,
Stories of old in night's stronghold.
A canvas painted with stars and grace,
Where every moment finds its place.

Muffled Dreams of the Cosmos

In the cradle of night, dreams intertwine,
Galaxies whisper through layers of time.
Muffled echoes of wishes and hopes,
Linger gently as the universe copes.

Nebulas swirl in soft, muted hues,
Crafting the path that our hearts choose.
Every star a story yet untold,
In the vastness, our destinies unfold.

Cradled in silence, we drift and float,
In cosmic seas, our thoughts denote.
Each dream a thread, interwoven tight,
Glowing softly in the heart of night.

Time stands still in this cosmic dance,
Illuminated paths of fate and chance.
In the depth of the universe's gleam,
We awaken to life, igniting the dream.

The Stillness Between Heartbeats

In the hush before breaths collide,
A pause where secrets hide.
Moments stretch in silent grace,
The world slows down, finding space.

Within the stillness, shadows dwell,
Echoes of stories we long to tell.
Time hangs lightly in tender threads,
Woven gently in the silence it spreads.

Every heartbeat a drum, a call,
In the quiet, we rise, we fall.
Caught between the moments, we see,
The beauty of what it means to be.

In this solitude, clarity blooms,
Filling the air with soft perfumes.
Awareness dawning in the night,
The stillness, a canvas of light.

Nightfall's Embrace

The day gives way to shadows deep,
As the world begins to sleep.
Night enfolds with a velvet hand,
Casting dreams across the land.

Stars awaken, a twinkling choir,
Lighting the paths of hearts aflire.
A gentle breeze whispers through trees,
Caressing the world with soothing ease.

In darkness, secrets shed their light,
Guiding souls through the quiet night.
Cradled softly in night's sweet grasp,
Each moment lingers, too precious to clasp.

Beneath the moon's watchful gaze,
Life unfolds in a dreamy haze.
In nightfall's embrace, we surrender,
To the magic of moments, tender and tender.

A Shroud of Peaceful Reflection

In the stillness of twilight's embrace,
Ripples of calm upon the lake's face.
Whispers of nature in soft refrain,
Cradling the world in a gentle chain.

Clouds blend with hues of a fading light,
Serenading thoughts that take flight.
Beneath the stars, dreams intertwine,
Finding solace in the divine.

Each moment draped in golden thread,
Echoes of laughter that gently spread.
The heart finds rhythm, the mind finds ease,
Nestled in moments that sweetly tease.

Leaves rustle softly, secrets shared,
Every breath taken, gently bared.
Time drips slowly, like melting ice,
Wrapped in the warmth of a quiet paradise.

As shadows deepen, the night unveils,
Stories of old carried by the gales.
Under the moon, we softly tread,
In a shroud of peace, our hearts are fed.

Shadows Dance in Partial Light

In the glow of a waning sun's rays,
Shadows twist and turn in playful ways.
Figures flit across the fading ground,
In their silent waltz, no judgments found.

Branches sway and whisper to the night,
Curtains of dusk bring an ethereal sight.
In the corners, secrets hide and tease,
Carried away with the soft, cool breeze.

Flickers of movement, a fleeting glance,
Inviting the world to join in the dance.
Twilight wraps the day in a cloak,
As laughter mingles with every joke.

The streetlamps light the paths we roam,
Illuminating the shadows back home.
Echoes of voices weave through the air,
Creating a tapestry, vibrant and rare.

Within the play of dark and light,
Life unfolds in the gentle night.
With every shadow that dips and sways,
Hope blooms anew in countless ways.

Beneath the Cloak of Nocturnal Grace

Underneath the cloak of midnight's grace,
Stars twinkle softly, a shimmering lace.
Moonlight spills forth, a silver stream,
Cradling the earth in a peaceful dream.

The world hushes deep in tranquil sighs,
As night unfurls her velvet skies.
Creatures stir in the comforting dark,
Each heartbeat echoes, a softened spark.

Gentle winds whisper through ancient trees,
Secrets carried on the playful breeze.
Nature's embrace, quiet and profound,
Beneath the stars, serenity found.

In the stillness, shadows softly play,
Painting the landscape in shades of gray.
Every glance skyward, a breath of hope,
In the embrace of night, our spirits cope.

With every moment, time seems to wane,
Filling our souls with unspoken gain.
Beneath the cloak, our fears take flight,
Wrapped in the magic of the night.

The Serenity of Falling Darkness

As daylight wanes and shadows grow,
A serene stillness begins to glow.
Embracing the dusk with open arms,
Wrapped in the night's calming charms.

The sky deepens into shades of blue,
Nature's canvas, a work anew.
With every star that appears to peek,
Whispers of dreams begin to speak.

Crickets serenade the softening air,
With sounds that linger, sweet and rare.
In the hush of twilight, hearts take rest,
Finding solace in moments blessed.

Night paints the world in a gentle hue,
Fading the worries of the day's queue.
Within this silence, we breathe alive,
In the embrace where our souls thrive.

As darkness falls, we're gently led,
To scattered thoughts, where hope is fed.
In the serene night, our spirits spark,
Emboldened by the grace in the dark.

Veiled in Soft Twilight

The sun dips down with grace,
Casting shadows on the ground.
Whispers echo through the trees,
As day surrenders without a sound.

The sky, a canvas painted pink,
With hues that softly blend and sway.
A gentle breeze begins to stir,
Bringing night where dreams can play.

Stars peek out with timid light,
Their brilliance cloaked in dusky haze.
Nightfall drapes the world in silk,
As time slows down in quiet ways.

Moonlight drifts on silver beams,
A lullaby for hearts that yearn.
The world is lost in tranquil thoughts,
As embers of the day now burn.

Within this tender, hushed embrace,
I find a peace that's deep and true.
Veiled in soft twilight's arms,
I think of all I long to do.

Stars That Hold Their Breath

In the vast expanse above,
Stars like secrets begin to gleam.
They sparkle softly in the night,
Hovering just beyond a dream.

A hush envelops all around,
As if the world has stopped to gaze.
Each twinkle a mysterious wish,
Lost within a cosmic maze.

Time seems paused in velvet air,
While shadows dance on midnight's stage.
They shimmer gently, hold their breath,
In a stellar, silent cage.

What stories do they long to share?
Of worlds unknown, of love and fate?
With every glimmer, secrets stir,
In darkness, hope will elevate.

Stars that watch with patient eyes,
Guide the heart through endless night.
In their glow, I find my path,
Cosmic whispers bring delight.

A Symphony of Quietude

The world is hushed, a gentle sigh,
As nature pauses, holds its breath.
In twilight's soft and sacred glow,
We find a moment, free from death.

Leaves murmur secrets to the wind,
Each rustle a soft, soothing tune.
The river hums a lullaby,
Beneath the watchful, waning moon.

A symphony of night unfolds,
Where silence weaves its perfect thread.
In every heartbeat close and clear,
The echoes of the past are fed.

Stars take notes in shards of light,
Each spark a part of night's refrain.
Melodies of dreams converge,
In sweet embrace, a soft champagne.

Within this tranquil, woven air,
I lose myself in all that's here.
A symphony, oh quietude,
Forever sings what hearts hold dear.

Ghosts of Dreams in the Dark

In the shadows where whispers dwell,
Ghosts of dreams begin to stir.
Flickers of hopes long tucked away,
In night's embrace, their voices purr.

Faded echoes of laughter ring,
In corners where memories bloom.
Those fleeting visions lace the air,
Like petals drifting in a room.

They wander through the velvet night,
Drifting softly, lost yet found.
Each heartbeat draws them closer still,
In silence, all their tales abound.

Whispers of what might have been,
Tangle in the cloak of dusk.
They tease the mind and dance around,
Like fragrant mist in twilight's musk.

In the dark, we meet again,
These phantoms wrapped in gentle light.
Ghosts of dreams, my faithful friends,
Together we take flight into night.

Whispers Carried on Midnight Winds

In the hush of night's soft glow,
Secrets dance where shadows flow.
Echoes of a distant call,
Carried gently, one and all.

Stars align with whispered grace,
Every twinkle finds its place.
Dreams unfurl like sails unfurled,
Guiding hearts through velvet world.

Crickets sing a lonesome tune,
Beneath the watchful eye of moon.
Breath of time, a fleeting sigh,
Drifting softly, passing by.

Stories wrote in silver light,
Granting solace in the night.
Every wish upon a star,
Closer to us, yet so far.

In the stillness, fears are shed,
Hope ignites from words unsaid.
Whispers linger, soft and clear,
Guiding souls through darkened sphere.

Still Waters of the Nighttime Heart

Beneath the quiet, deep and wide,
Secrets of the heart abide.
Ripples dance on silent streams,
Reflecting all our fleeting dreams.

Starry skies and whispered sighs,
Cradle all our heartfelt ties.
In the dark, the shadows part,
Revealing stillness of the heart.

Every heartbeat, calm and slow,
Carries tales that ebb and flow.
Like the moon on water's bed,
Gentle thoughts begin to spread.

Silent prayers drift through the night,
Illuminated by soft light.
In still waters, peace we find,
Comfort flows, untainted mind.

Whispers soft, like evening's breath,
Captivate the dance of death.
Yet in stillness, life awakes,
With every wave, the heart remakes.

The Soft Footfall of a Dream

Like a feather on the breeze,
Dreams arrive with gentle ease.
Hushed arrival, light and sweet,
Stirring echoes of our beat.

Floating softly, soft and pure,
In our hearts, they find a cure.
Painted skies and velvet hue,
Whispers promise, something new.

Every step, a tale to share,
Guiding hearts with tender care.
In the silence, dreams take flight,
Illuminated by the night.

Through the shadows, colors blend,
Every note, a life to mend.
In the stillness, truths appear,
Whispers of what we hold dear.

Finding meaning in the dark,
Dreams ignite with hopeful spark.
Soft footfalls on the ground,
In this realm, yet lost, yet found.

Nightfall's Embrace on Wandering Souls

As the day gives in to night,
Wandering souls seek the light.
In shadows deep, they find their way,
Guided by the stars that play.

Embrace of dusk, a tender hold,
Filling hearts with stories old.
With every breath, the world stands still,
In the dark, dreams begin to thrill.

Voices softly intertwine,
In the deep where spirits shine.
Light and shadow softly sway,
Painting paths of night and day.

Through the dark, the whispers seek,
Hearts that ache and souls that speak.
Nightfall's promise, bright and warm,
Bringing solace, safe from harm.

With each heartbeat, wisdom flows,
In night's arms, the journey grows.
Wandering souls find rest tonight,
In the beauty of starlit light.

The Unfurling of Dusk's Whisper

A hush falls soft as day departs,
The sky blushes with fading light.
Whispers of night play hidden parts,
As shadows dance and dreams take flight.

Starlight begins its tender gleam,
While silence wraps the world in grace.
The gentle folds of a twilight dream,
Invite the heart to slow its pace.

Crickets serenade the dark,
A symphony of dusk unfolds.
The fireflies flicker their tiny spark,
In this calm rest, the night beholds.

Time drapes low with golden thread,
Each moment stretches, soft and wide.
In the cloak of night, fears are shed,
And in its arms, the soul can bide.

Upon this canvas deep and vast,
Nature's hymn resounds anew.
The beauty of the fading past,
In dusk's embrace, we find our view.

Calmed by the Night's Gentle Breath

The moon sits bright in velvet skies,
Casting shadows, soft and mild.
A gentle breeze, a sweet surprise,
Whispers secrets, unbeguiled.

Stars twinkle like dreams in the night,
Winking softly from above.
In this calm, each worry takes flight,
Embraced by the night, we're wrapped in love.

Trees sway lightly, a rhythmic dance,
Leaves murmur tales of days gone by.
In such stillness, we find our chance,
To pause and breathe, to simply sigh.

The world sighs deep as darkness falls,
Resting from its daily race.
In twilight's arms, each echo calls,
Inviting hearts to find their place.

Nature breathes in perfect sync,
As thoughts unwind and freely roam.
In this embrace, we softly sink,
Finding peace, we call it home.

A Tapestry Woven in Quietude

In the fabric of night, we weave,
Threads of silence, soft and light.
Each moment's touch, let us believe,
Creates a tapestry of night.

Whispers linger, secrets shared,
In the stillness, hearts connect.
Every breath, a gift declared,
In quietude, we find respect.

Stars are stitches in the sky,
Glowing softly through the dark.
In such beauty, dreams can fly,
Every spark, a glowing mark.

Embers of dusk, softly glow,
Painting skies with hues divine.
In the calm, our spirits flow,
Woven patterns closely align.

As dawn approaches, threads entwine,
The night whispers its last embrace.
In this art, our souls combine,
A tapestry of love and grace.

The Starlit Silence of Forgotten Paths

Moonlight bathes the winding trails,
A gentle hush, the night sincere.
Each step echoes with ancient tales,
In the quiet, we draw near.

Stars guide us through the shadowed lanes,
Their twinkling glimmers light the way.
In silence deep, where peace remains,
We wander freely, hearts at play.

Every rustle, a story told,
A memory cloaked in night's embrace.
The air is crisp, the world unfolds,
As we explore this sacred space.

Time feels still, as moments blend,
With each breath, we become alive.
On forgotten paths, we find a friend,
Within the silence, we revive.

The night wraps all in softest care,
Binding us to the stars above.
In its embrace, we shed despair,
And walk our paths, wrapped in love.

The Quiet Between Heartbeats

In silence deep, we find the grace,
A space where time must slow its pace.
Each heartbeat whispers, soft and low,
In this hush, our truest selves glow.

Moments linger, fragile yet bright,
A fleeting touch, a spark of light.
Between the beats, a world unfolds,
With stories whispered, dreams retold.

The breath of life, a gentle sigh,
In shadows cast, our hopes can fly.
In stillness dwells a sacred song,
Echoes of where our hearts belong.

With every pause, we learn to feel,
The weight of love, the art of real.
In quietude, we see the thread,
That binds us all, the words unsaid.

So let us cherish every beat,
The spaces where our hearts do meet.
In tranquil moments, we find peace,
A symphony that will not cease.

Celestial Revelations

Beneath the night, the stars ignite,
Whispers of worlds in silver light.
Each twinkle tells a tale profound,
A dance of dreams, both lost and found.

In cosmic realms, the secrets swirl,
Galaxies spin, a timeless whirl.
The moonlight paints a path so clear,
Guiding our hopes, diminishing fear.

Celestial fires, the heavens weave,
In every spark, we dare believe.
Our wishes cast, like ships at sea,
Adrift in space, we yearn to be.

With every dawn, the promise wakes,
A canvas bright, the heart it stakes.
In revelations, we find our place,
In this vastness, we share embrace.

So gaze above, let wonder swell,
In cosmic truths, our spirits dwell.
The universe sings, a timeless song,
In revelations, we all belong.

The Drumbeat of Stillness

In the hush of dawn, a heartbeat plays,
The drumbeat of stillness, in gentle ways.
Each moment stretches, like shadows cast,
In quiet rhythms, our souls are amassed.

The world may rush, but here we stand,
In tranquil peace, we clasp our hands.
The pulse of life, in whispers clear,
In stillness, we find what we hold dear.

The echoing heartbeat, a firm embrace,
In soothing tones, we find our place.
Through silence, we hear the stories told,
In gentle prisms, our hearts unfold.

Each breath a beat, a soft refrain,
In stillness wrapped, we ease our pain.
With every moment, the world alights,
In the drumbeat's pulse, the heart ignites.

Embrace the calm that silence brings,
In stillness, we are the truest kings.
The drumbeat whispers, let it be,
In quietude, we are forever free.

Night's Lullaby for Dreamers

As stars unveil their silken glow,
The night wraps dreams in a tender flow.
With every sigh, the world takes pause,
In moonlit grace, we find the cause.

A lullaby sung by the softest breeze,
Whispers of hope that put hearts at ease.
In shadows deep, our wishes soar,
As night enfolds, we yearn for more.

The dreams take flight, on gentle wings,
In twilight's arms, the magic clings.
Each heartbeat echoes a timeless tune,
A serenade beneath the moon.

So close your eyes, let worries fade,
In night's embrace, the fears degrade.
With every whisper, the stars align,
In dreams, dear heart, our souls entwine.

Beneath the sky, let spirits roam,
In night's sweet song, we find our home.
In every lullaby, the heart finds cheer,
As dreamers dance, the world feels near.

Stars as Silent Sentinels

High above, they silently gleam,
Guardians of our midnight dream.
Each twinkle tells a story old,
Whispers in the night unfold.

In velvet skies, their watch begins,
As silver beams caress our sins.
A cosmic dance, both bright and bold,
The secrets of the night retold.

They flicker soft, like eyes from far,
Reminding us we're not ajar.
A sea of light, our hearts they fill,
With hopes and dreams that time stands still.

Through galaxies, they weave their threads,
A tapestry where all are led.
With every wish, we cast our fate,
Sentinels that never wait.

Embrace the night, let wonders flow,
With silent stars, our spirits grow.
In their embrace, we find our way,
As night transforms to break of day.

The Pause Before Dawn

In stillness hangs the darkest hour,
The world asleep, yet feels the power.
A breath held tight, the night holds on,
Awaiting light, the stars are gone.

Shadows linger, whispers fade,
Time feels frozen, dreams are made.
The horizon blushes, soft and light,
As night reluctantly takes flight.

In this moment, hearts unite,
A tranquil peace, a gentle sight.
Birds begin their morning song,
In the silence, we belong.

A secret pact between the sky,
And all that stirs, both low and high.
Mysteries in the twilight haze,
Await the sun's first golden rays.

Hold your breath and feel the change,
As the world starts to rearrange.
The pause before the dawn takes flight,
A fleeting dance of day and night.

Night's Hidden Harmony

In shadows deep, the silence hums,
A melody through darkness drums.
The rustling leaves, the cool night air,
Compose a score beyond compare.

Soft crickets play their serenade,
While owls call from the quiet glade.
Each sound a note in nature's song,
A symphony where all belong.

The moonlight bathes the world in gold,
A silver thread in night's enfold.
With every breath, the harmony grows,
In whispered tones, the magic flows.

The stars align, a cosmic beat,
In the stillness, hearts skip a beat.
Unseen rhythms guide our way,
In night's embrace, we choose to stay.

Beneath the vast, enchanting dome,
In hidden sounds, we find our home.
Embrace the night, let music throng,
In night's hidden harmony, we belong.

Silence Wrapped in Moonlight

A gentle hush, the world stands still,
Wrapped in moonlight, dreams fulfill.
Soft shadows weave, as twilight glows,
In the silence, peace bestows.

Each silver beam a touch so light,
Guiding souls through endless night.
Whispers linger, secrets kept,
In moonlit thoughts, our spirits leapt.

The stillness wraps like a warm embrace,
In this calm, we find our place.
Beneath the gaze of silent stars,
We heal our wounds, forget the scars.

A moment shared, hearts intertwined,
In the quiet, a bond defined.
With every breath, the night perceives,
In moonlit dreams, our heart believes.

So let us dwell in shadows bright,
For silence speaks in the soft night.
Wrapped in moonlight's tender sway,
In tranquil stillness, we shall stay.

The Weight of Quietude

In the stillness, thoughts reside,
Wrapped in velvet, dreams abide.
Whispers dance upon the air,
Echoes linger, free from care.

Time drips slowly, like sweet wine,
Fleeting moments that intertwine.
A gentle sigh, a soft refrain,
Melodies within the brain.

Faintest laughter rides the breeze,
As nature hums with perfect ease.
In this realm, all burdens fade,
Calm descends, fears are outweighed.

Holding heartbeats near and tight,
Finding solace in the night.
The weight of quiet wraps around,
In silence, true peace is found.

Stars above begin to blink,
Guiding thoughts to pause and think.
In the hush, we learn to be,
Weightless souls, wild and free.

Chasing Shadows at Dusk

The sun dips low, a fiery sphere,
Casting shadows far and near.
With every step, the dusk draws near,
Chasing dreams with no fear.

Hues of orange paint the sky,
Whispers of night start to pry.
Silhouettes dance, the world awakes,
In twilight's grasp, the silence breaks.

Footprints linger on the ground,
Stories of lives, once profound.
Through the mist, we run and spin,
Chasing shadows, hearts set to win.

Moments slip like grains of sand,
Drifting softly, close at hand.
In this chase, we find our place,
Embraced by dusk's tender grace.

The night will fall, yet we remain,
In every shadow, there's no pain.
For in this chase, we truly find,
The light that lingers in the mind.

Among the Stars

Beneath a canopy of night,
We find the stars, a guiding light.
In every twinkle, tales unfold,
Of dreams once dreamt, and hearts so bold.

With every glance, a wish is tossed,
No moment spent shall be lost.
In the vastness, souls collide,
Among the stars, we softly glide.

Galaxies swirl in cosmic dance,
Inviting hearts to take a chance.
The universe sings a lullaby,
Underneath the endless sky.

Whispers echo through the night,
Each spark ignites a spark of light.
Boundless dreams, forever soar,
Among the stars, we yearn for more.

Together in this vast embrace,
Connected through time and space.
Among the stars, we'll always stay,
Finding magic in our way.

We Pause

In moments where the world stands still,
We pause to catch a breath, a thrill.
Time shifts gently, like a stream,
Here in stillness, we find a dream.

The heart beats softly in the hush,
A tranquil sense replaces rush.
With every sigh, we let it go,
Embracing quiet, letting flow.

In fleeting glances, truth awakes,
As stillness wraps, the spirit breaks.
We weave the threads of the unknown,
Finding comfort in the lone.

In this pause, we breathe and glean,
A canvas painted, fresh and green.
From chaos birthed, to calm anew,
In every silence, find what's true.

With open hearts and open minds,
In this moment, peace we find.
Together we shall rise and pause,
In life's spiral, love is the cause.

Celestial Whispers

In twilight's glow, the stars align,
Celestial whispers, soft and fine.
They tell of journeys yet to come,
Of quiet hearts and beating drums.

Moonbeams brush the leaves so light,
Guiding dreams through endless night.
Each twinkle sings a song of old,
In distant galaxies, tales unfold.

A symphony of worlds beyond,
The universe, our hearts respond.
Through cosmic winds, we drift and flow,
Find solace in what we don't know.

With every pulse, the heavens speak,
Echoing dreams that we all seek.
Celestial whispers, sweet and clear,
Remind us of all we hold dear.

So let us listen, hearts aglow,
To the wisdom that stars bestow.
In silent night, we write our fate,
To celestial whispers, we relate.

In the Embrace of Darkness

In shadows deep, silence reigns,
Whispers weave through hollow chains.
Moonlight flickers, soft and bright,
Guiding lost souls through the night.

Echoes dance upon the ground,
Voices call without a sound.
Stars above, a guiding spark,
Holding hands in the dark.

Fear dissolves, as dreams awake,
In the stillness, hearts do ache.
A gentle touch upon the skin,
Inviting warmth to slip within.

In this realm where shadows play,
Time seems to drift and sway.
Every heartbeat sings a tune,
While the night breathes of the moon.

With every sigh, the darkness holds,
A tapestry of dreams unfolds.
In this place, we find our peace,
In the dark, our fears decrease.

Serenity's Lullaby

The gentle breeze hums a song,
In the quiet where we belong.
Softly drifting, the world slows,
In this calm, our spirit glows.

Stars above keep watchful gaze,
Guiding us through twilight's haze.
Whispers of night, sweet and low,
Serenity's lullaby flows.

The ocean's waves kiss the shore,
A soothing rhythm we adore.
In the stillness, hearts rejoice,
Listening close to nature's voice.

Dreams unfurl like petals bright,
In the embrace of the night.
Crickets sing their soft refrain,
In this moment, love remains.

The world fades, and we are one,
Underneath the watchful sun.
In serenity, our hearts claim,
Peaceful whispers, love's sweet name.

Shadows Dance in Twilight

As twilight falls, the shadows sway,
Fading light turns night to play.
With every flicker, stories told,
In the dusk, the magic unfolds.

Figures waltz in whispered tones,
As the moonlight softly moans.
The breeze carries a tender kiss,
In the dark, we find our bliss.

Echoes linger, memories spin,
Inviting warmth from deep within.
Dancing shadows, fleeting grace,
In this moment, we embrace.

The horizon blushes, time stands still,
As the heart seeks its sweet thrill.
Stars awaken, a dance begins,
While the night softly spins.

In twilight's charm, we drift away,
Where shadows dance and hearts can stay.
Lost in the wonder, we feel alive,
In the twilight, our spirits thrive.

Soft Breath of the Midnight Hour

A stillness cloaks the midnight hour,
As time surrenders to the power.
The world asleep, yet dreams awake,
In the hush, our hearts will break.

Moonbeams cast their silver light,
Over landscapes draped in night.
Whispers weave through the air,
In this moment, free of care.

Gentle sighs the night extends,
As a lullaby softly bends.
Stars glimmer like lost memories,
Carried on a midnight breeze.

The heart's rhythm, calm and deep,
Guides our souls as they gently leap.
In the darkness, love ignites,
Fueling the dreams that the heart invites.

A soft breath fills the space around,
With every heartbeat, peace is found.
In the silence, we shall dance,
Lost forever in love's trance.

The Unwritten Stories of the Dark

In shadows deep, where whispers dwell,
Old tales linger, secrets swell.
Each breath holds echoes, soft and stark,
The unwritten stories of the dark.

Lost are the voices, the fates they trace,
In hidden corners, time leaves no space.
A canvas blank, with strokes of night,
Lives intertwined, yet out of sight.

Flickering dreams in the stillness grow,
Beneath the surface, ancient flow.
Beneath the stars, they quietly spark,
The unwritten stories of the dark.

Mysteries clad in a shroud of hope,
Weaving through shadows, our hearts elope.
Together we wander, igniting the spark,
In the tapestry spun by the dark.

Like paper boats on a silent stream,
Each moment captured, a fleeting dream.
In silence profound, we leave our mark,
The unwritten stories of the dark.

Gentle Flickers in the Great Abyss

In realms of boundless night they hide,
Gentle flickers that softly bide.
Each twinkling star, a whisper clear,
In the great abyss, hope draws near.

They dance with grace, in cosmic swirl,
A symphony forged, as cosmos twirl.
Amidst the silence, they catch our eye,
Gentle flickers in the endless sky.

Their warmth ignites the cold embrace,
Guiding lost souls with tender grace.
In every blink, a story spun,
These gentle flickers, a world begun.

In vast expanse where dreams reside,
They shimmer softly, foreverslide.
A beacon of light, ever so spry,
Gentle flickers in the arms of night.

Through cosmic depths, they find their flight,
In the heart of darkness, pure delight.
A silent promise, pure as air,
Gentle flickers, ever fair.

Moonbeams Pouring Into Solitude

Through velvet skies, the moonlight spills,
Softly tracing the silent hills.
Whispers of silver, dreams unfold,
Moonbeams pouring into solitude.

In quiet corners where shadows play,
The heart finds solace, come what may.
In every glimmer, warmth is found,
Moonbeams pouring without a sound.

They touch the earth with a gentle grace,
Filling the void, a sweet embrace.
In the hush of night, all fears elude,
Moonbeams pouring into solitude.

Casting light on what's left unseen,
The essence glows in the serene.
A soft reminder, fierce yet crude,
Moonbeams pouring, spirits renewed.

With each soft breath, time slows its flight,
As dreams awaken in pale twilight.
A tender promise, pure and true,
Moonbeams pouring, renewed view.

Midnight's Secret Language

In the cradle of night, whispers blend,
A secret language with no end.
Stars in chorus, soft and grand,
Midnight's secrets hand in hand.

Words unspoken, feelings shared,
Every glance, a bond declared.
Through the darkness, spirits range,
In the stillness, we find change.

A symphony of silence plays,
Painting visions in gentle rays.
Melodies linger, sweet and strange,
The magic found in midnight's language.

Within the quiet, hearts convene,
Dreams become the unseen scene.
In shadowed moments, hearts exchange,
The whispers held in midnight's range.

Like ancient texts in a faded tome,
Each heartbeat echoes, leading home.
In every pause, the thoughts rearrange,
Midnight's secret language, vast and strange.